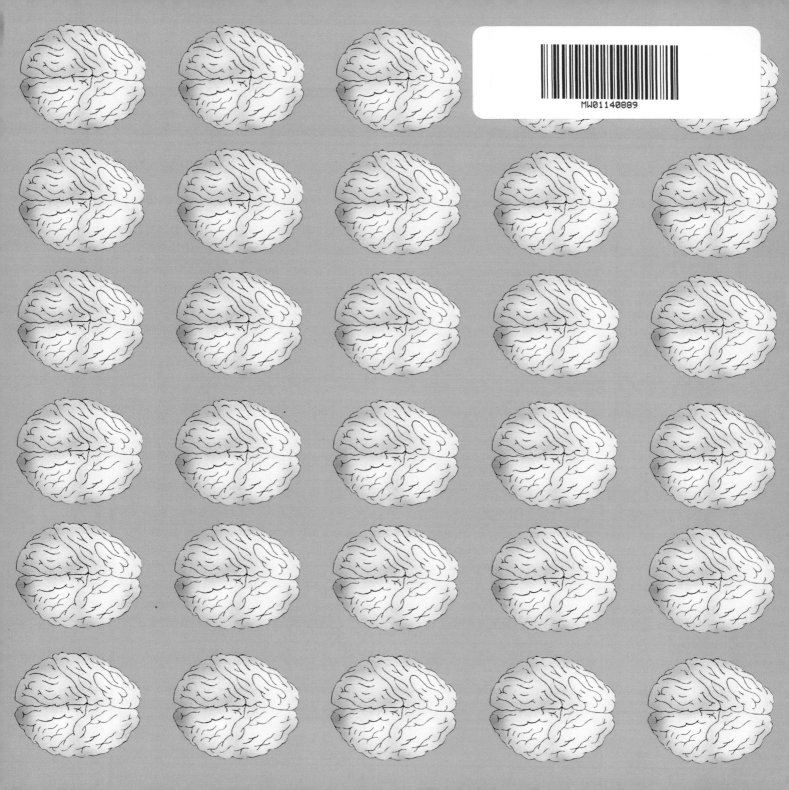

MW01140889

Bean Water Publishing

Copyright © 2017 Alyssa Andres and Kristina C. Andres
All rights reserved.
ISBN-13: 978-1546720904
ISBN-10: 1546720901

Story by Alyssa Andres

Art by Kristina C. Andres

To the diverse young minds
shaping tomorrow...

Ladies and gentlemen, grab a seat on the train. It's time to tour the magnificent brain!

My friends call me Neuron
and I am a cell.
I deliver messages in the brain,
and I do this well!

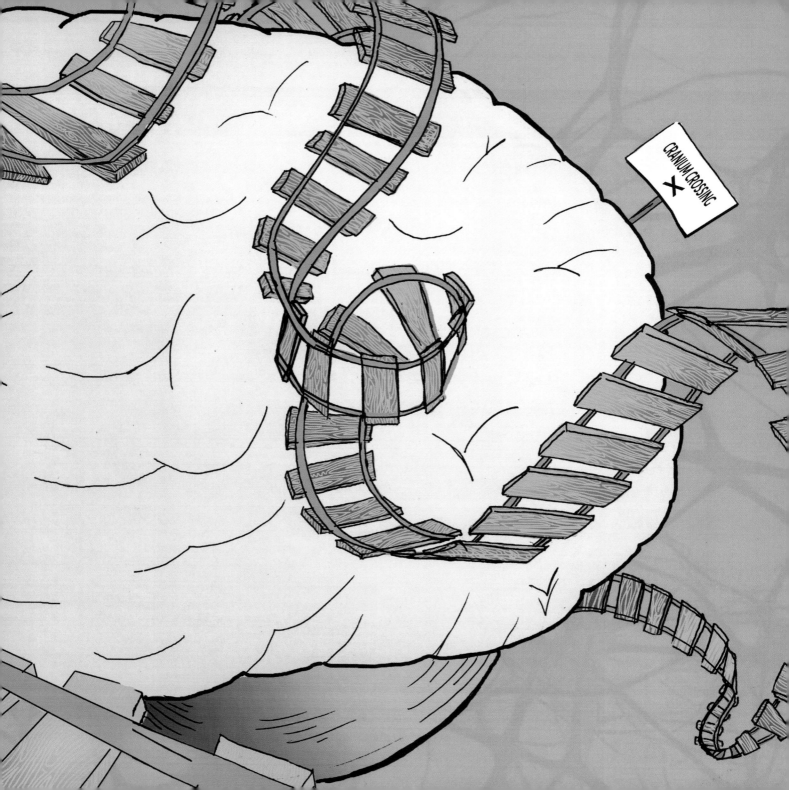

Now straight down this track,
and around this turn,
you'll see the frontal lobe:
the place where you learn.

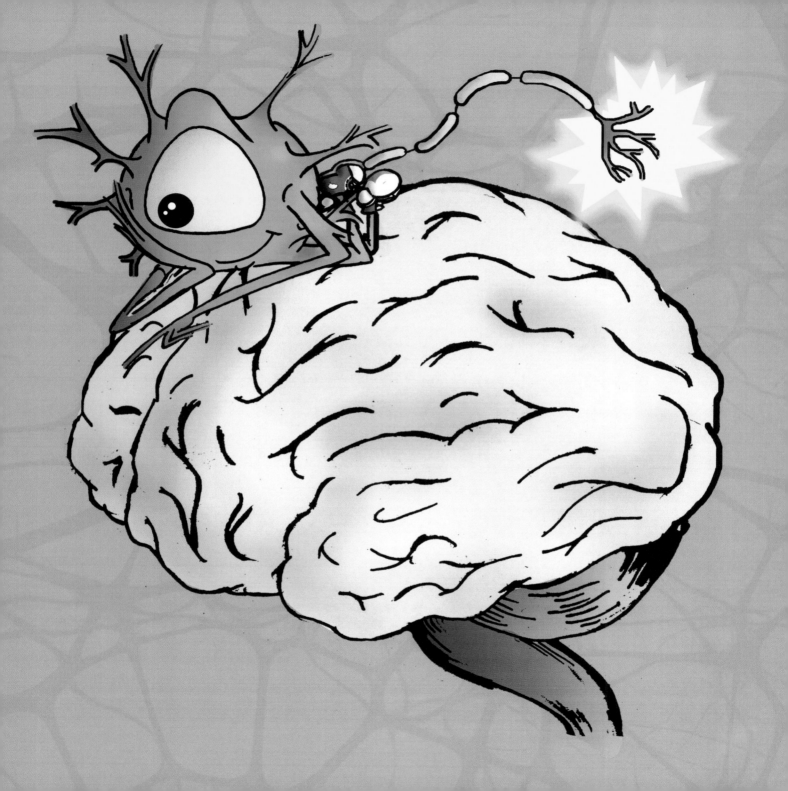

The frontal lobe's busy.
It never gets rest.

It helps you make
smart decisions,
and study for tests.

The temporal lobe!
Look and see!
Look and see!
It's the reason you have
such a great memory.

The temporal lobe
has a big job to do.

It allows you to hear
all the sounds around you.

Let's stop here for tea.
That should hit the spot.
The parietal lobe says,
"that tea is too hot!"

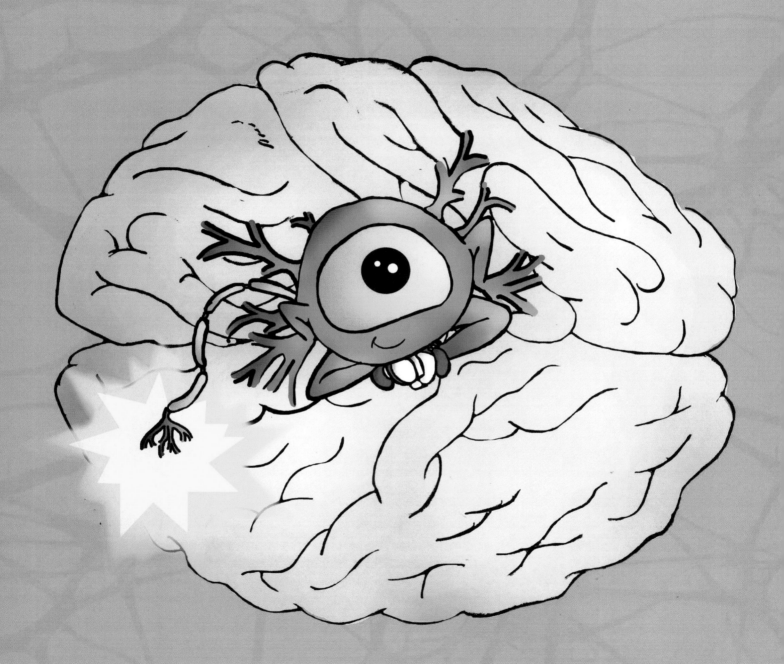

Your senses: touch and taste,
live happily here.

With no parietal lobe,
they would all disappear...

The last stop for today
is the back of your head.
The occipital lobe rests
when you go to bed.

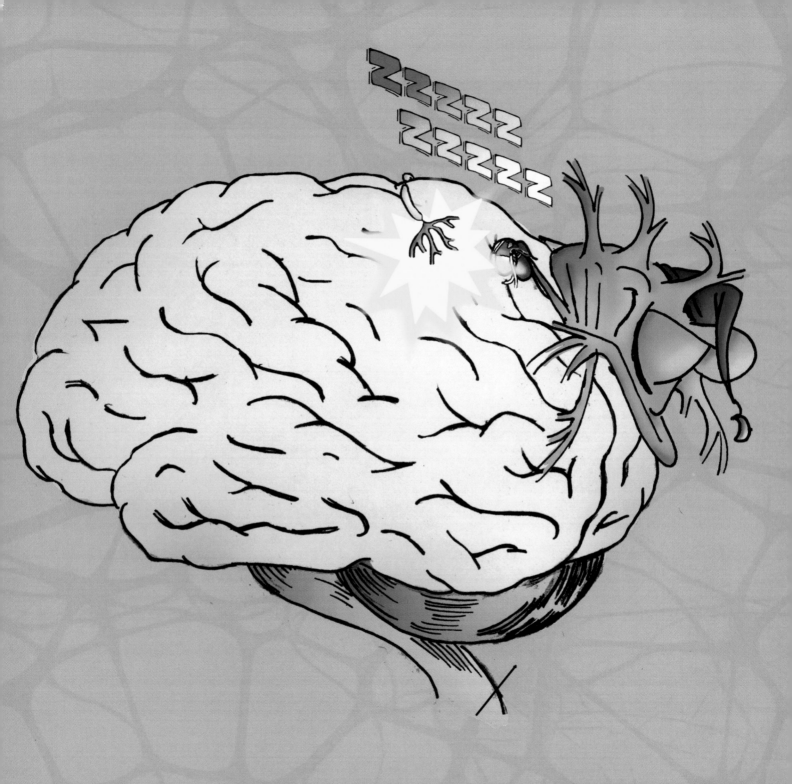

When you open
your eyes
and see friends
or a tree,
you can thank
this lobe
for helping
you see.

Your brain is special.
It shapes who you are,
whether you become a doctor,
an athlete,
or a famous rockstar.

Be sure to take care of your brain every day.

Wear a helmet,

eat healthy,

and be kind always.

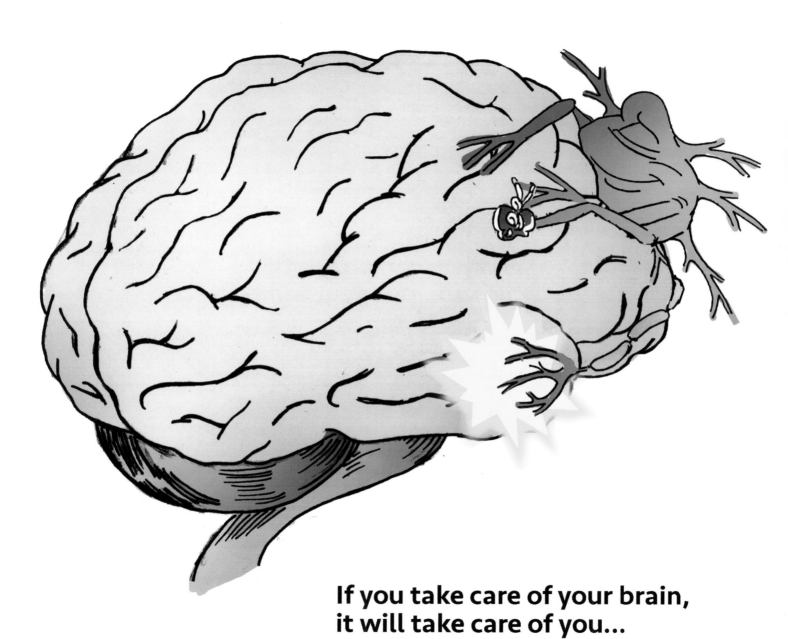

If you take care of your brain,
it will take care of you...

and you can do anything,
that you put your mind to.

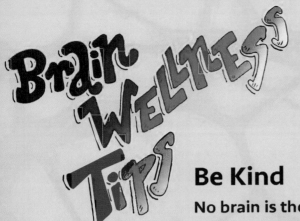

Be Kind

No brain is the same. We won't always agree;
but we are all equal, so kindness is key.

Eat Healthy

When our tummy is hungry and needs something to eat,
have veggies or proteins, not sugary treats.

Be Active

Jump off the couch. There's so much to do...
Play outside, run around: this is better for you.

Meditate

Sit down somewhere silent. Breathe in and breathe out.
Having time to relax, is what this is about.

Learn

Read books and listen. Keep a wide open mind.
Oh, the things you will learn and the things you will find.

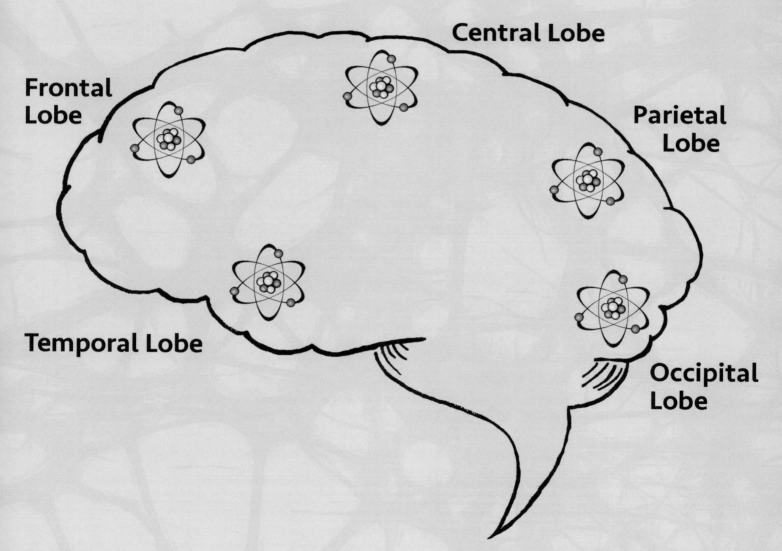

Alyssa Andres is a PhD student of integrative medicine and quantum physics. She is the founder of the Mind Body Lab, specializing in brainwave optimization. She currently lives and works in Victoria, British Columbia.

To learn more about Alyssa and Mind Body Lab, follow @alysssandres or @mindbodylab on Instagram.

Kristina C. Andres is an author and illustrator currently living in Victoria British Columbia. She teaches high school Art and English. Her second book "Zombie Makes Three" will be released in 2017.

To learn more about Kristina and her upcoming projects, follow @kristina.c.andres on Instagram.

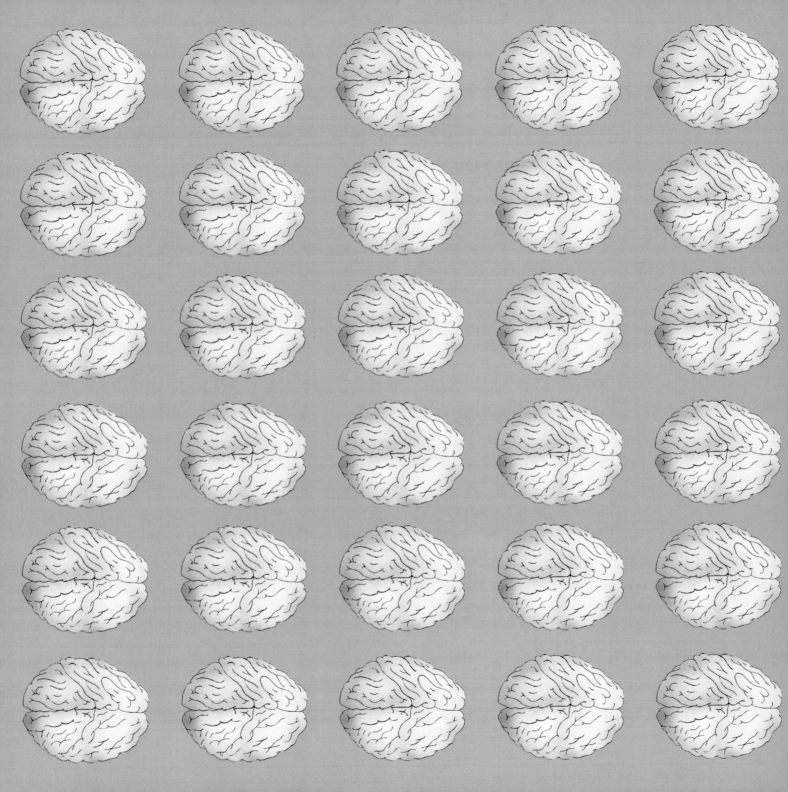

75085898R00023

Made in the USA
Columbia, SC
11 August 2017